Religion, morality and knowledge
being necessary to good government
and the happiness of mankind,
schools and the means of education
shall forever be encouraged.

The Northwest Ordinance of 1787,
Papers of the Continental Congress No.59

First published in 1994 by
Brompton Books Corp.,
15 Sherwood Place,
Greenwich, CT 06830
USA

Copyright © 1994 Brompton Books Corp.

ISBN 1-85841-107-6

Printed in China

The University of
MICHIGAN

A Seasonal Portrait

Brompton

Introduction

The words "the University of Michigan" always bring to mind traditional images of campus: lecture halls filled with students, get-togethers in dorm rooms, spirited classroom discussions, students toiling away in the library . . . or perhaps out protesting on the Diag.

Thoughts of Michigan also call up some very personal images for many. Some treasure memories of walking through the falling leaves on a marvelous autumn afternoon to Michigan Stadium, becoming one of 105,000 fans thrilling to the excitement of a Michigan game with the Wolverines and the Michigan Marching Band giving their best. Some proudly recall sharing in the special moment of a Rose Bowl victory or an NCAA Basketball Championship game. Others look back on the cultural richness of Michigan, with memories of great orchestras and artists performing in Hill Auditorium and of the profusion of student and professional productions and performances—the wealth of drama, music, art, dance, film, and opera that makes Ann Arbor such a vibrant and cosmopolitan community.

There is the Michigan that serves as the youthful conscience of a nation, the site of the first Teach-Ins, the first Earth Day, the home of the 100-year-old *Michigan Daily*, engaging students in so many of the critical issues of the day. And there is the caring Michigan, serving almost one million patients each year at the University of Michigan Medical Center, one of the world's great centers of medical research, teaching, and treatment.

There is Michigan, a university of the world, long renowned as a truly international center of learning. Walk down the streets of any capital city in the world and you will find her graduates, more often than not, in positions of leadership. Indeed, Michigan is even a university "of the universe," with a chapter of the UM Alumni Association on the moon, established by the crew of Apollo 15, all Michigan alums!

Since its founding, the University of Michigan has been regarded as the flagship of public higher education in America. A century ago, the University provided leadership by laying the foundation for the modern research university. Michigan was the first public university to introduce professional education in medicine, engineering, law, and teaching. Its impact on the development of new programs and disciplines in American higher education has been extraordinary; its lists of firsts in both academic programs and research would run for many pages.

But it may be that Michigan's greatest contribution to American education is its commitment to provide, in President James B. Angell's words, "an uncommon education for the common man," an education as good as any available in the world, an education for all with the ability and will to succeed, regardless of race, creed, and economic background. In many ways it was at the University of Michigan that Thomas Jefferson's enlightened dreams for the public university were most fully realized.

The University of Michigan has a remarkable ability to touch our lives. In just the few short years that we spend on campus, we become a part of the Michigan family. In our hearts, Ann Arbor is forever after our home, and our lives are shaped by our Michigan experience. The Michigan tradition becomes a unifying force that links us together through alumni activities and involvement across America and around the world.

Our images of this marvelous University are formed by the many different ways in which it has touched our own lives. There is no one way to capture the excitement of Michigan, to take the measure of all that it does and all that it stands for as an institution. This photographic essay portrays the University through an array of images, timeless in nature, representing the great traditions of the past and visions of the future. As these images flow through the seasons, from the excitement of new students arriving in the fall, through the sparkling images of winter, to spring and commencement, and finally the explosion of color in a Michigan summer, we all gain a better appreciation of the life and impact of this extraordinary institution.

(overleaf) Regents Plaza

another school year begins. . .

8.   Law School overlooking South University Street

Michigan Union overlooking Daedalus, sculpture by Charles Ginnever at Museum of Art 9.

10.   The Diag and Hatcher Graduate Library

Burton Memorial Tower rising above the trees at Michigan League   11.

12.   Institute of Science and Technology

Dana Building   13.

14. Rackham School of Graduate Studies

Senator Carl Levin with Presidential candidate Bill Clinton and wife, Hillary   15.

16.   Burton Memorial Tower

18.   Museum of Art

20.   North Campus Diag

Electrical Engineering and Computer Science Atrium 21.

22.   Palmer Field

24.   "Hail to the Victors!"

33.

The Michigan Marching Band

36.   Angell Hall

38.   Legal Research, Law School

Courtyard at Executive Residence, School of Business Administration   39.

40.   School of Education

42.   Michigan Union

44.   Ruthven Museums

46. Rackham School of Graduate Studies

Angell Hall Computing Center   47.
(overleaf) The Diag

50. Stockwell Hall

52.   East Quadrangle

54.   Sundial at School of Music

56.   Michigan Stadium

58. Legal Research, Law School

60.   Clements Library

62. School of Art

64.   Hill Auditorium

Messiah Concert, Hill Auditorium 65.

Legendary Artists of the World Stage
at Hill Auditorium

66.   (above) Itzhak Perlman, Pinchas Zuckerman
(right) Leonard Bernstein

(left) Jessye Norman
(below) Eugene Ormandy, Vladimir Horowitz

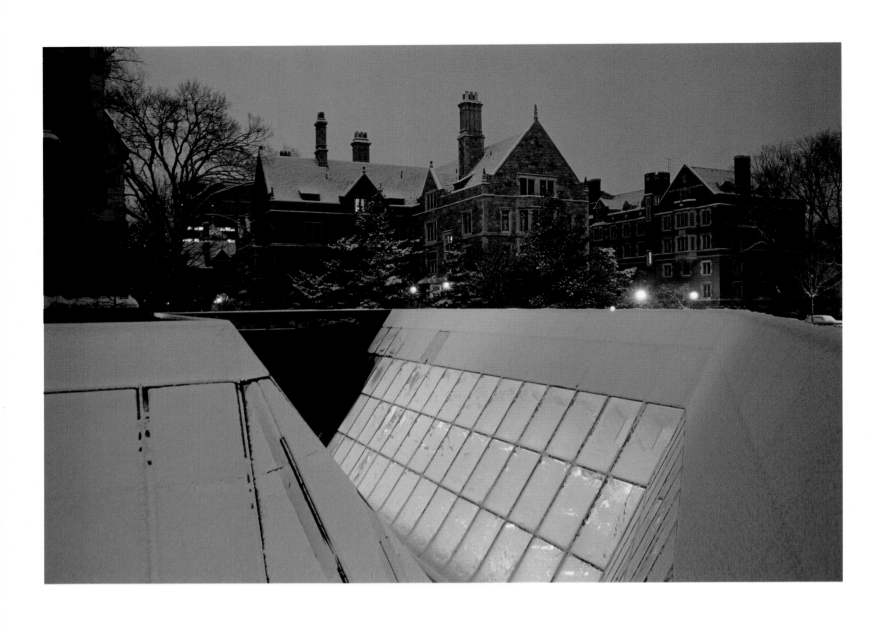

68.   Smith Law Library with Law School and Martha Cook Residence Hall

70.   Alumni Center

School of Business Administration   71.

74.   Coach Steve Fisher and the Fab Five

76.   Crisler Arena

78.   Yost Arena

80.   Canham Natatorium

84.   Hatcher Graduate Library overlooking the Diag

Michigan Union overlooking Regents Plaza and "The Cube," untitled sculpture by Bernard Rosenthal   85.

86.   Willard Henry Dow Laboratory

88.   Michigan League Courtyard

90.   Detroit Observatory

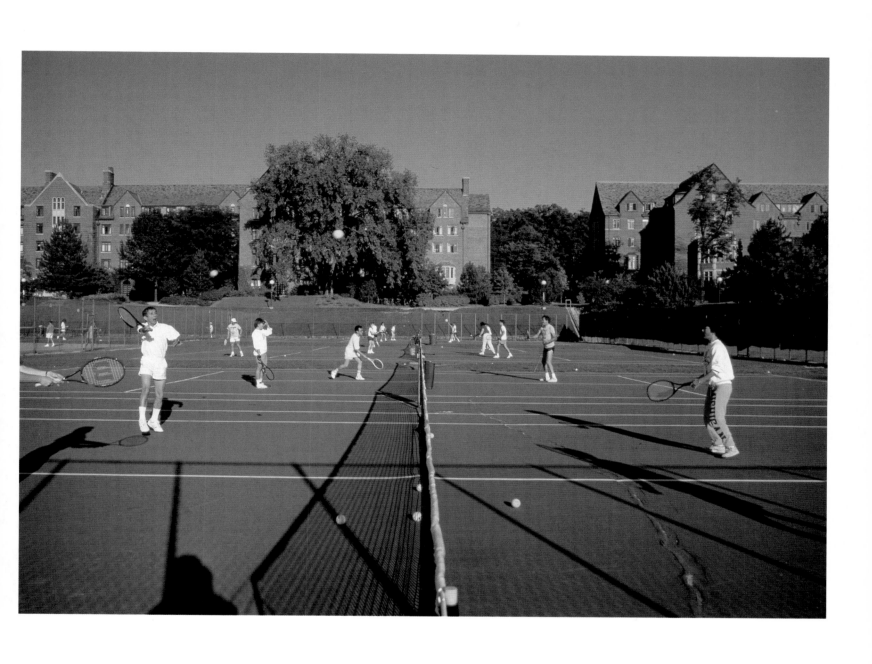

Palmer Field in front of Mosher-Jordan and Stockwell   91.

94.　　"The Rock"

United States President George Bush   101.

Peony garden in Nichols Arboretum   103.

104.   Hill Auditorium and Burton Memorial Tower overlooking Ingalls Mall

Fountain, *Sunday Morning in Deep Waters* by Carl Milles, on Ingalls Mall   105.

106.   Dennison Physics and Astronomy

108.   Bronze statue, *Eve*, by Paul Suttman, on the lawn of Martha Cook

110.   School of Nursing

School of Dentistry   111.

112.   Rackham School of Graduate Studies

"Top of the Park" at Power Center for the Performing Arts   113.

114.   Hatcher Graduate Library

Kresge Business Library and Executive Residence at School of Business Administration   115.

116.   University of Michigan Hospitals on Huron River

118.   Sculpture, *Summaries of Arithmetic Through Dust, Including Writing Not Yet Printed*
       by Alice Aycock, at College of Engineering

National competition-winning solar car *Sunrunner* and its student team   119.

120.   Gerald R. Ford Library

122.   School of Music

124.   Matthaei Botanical Gardens

126.   *. . . and it begins again.*

127.

This book is the result of the efforts of a number of talented photographers, whose work (credited below) captures so well the spirit of the University of Michigan. We are particularly grateful to Sydney L. Mayer '62, '63 MA, the president of Brompton Books, for his generosity, insight, and dedication to his alma mater. Lynn Leedy '59, '64 MA, Brompton Books, was instrumental in bringing about the publication of this work. We are grateful for all of her efforts.

But this book most of all, owes its vitality to Anne Duderstadt and Liene Karels, whose vision, industry, creativity, and judgment made this book possible. As editors and designers of this book, it is their spirit that truly informs it.

Photographers:
Joseph Abbeduto – 124, 125
Duane Black – 72, 73, (top) 74
Philip Dattilo – 9, 12, 14, 16, 18-23, 36-39, 41-47, 50, 52, 57, 59, 61-63, 68-71, 86, 87, 90, 96, 102, 105, 114, 115, 122, 123, 126, 127
Steve Kagan – (top, right, bottom) 98
Robert Kalmbach – 77, 92, 93, (upper) 100, 119
Per Kjeldsen – i, 8, 10, 11, 13, 15, 17, 24-35, 51, 54-56, 60, 64-66, (bottom) 74, 75, 78-80, 84, 85, 88, 89, 91, 94, 95, 103, 104, 106-113, 118, 120, 121
Sara Krulwich – (left) 98, (center) 99
Larime Photographic – 116, 117
Randall Mascharka – 76
Dean Russell – 40
Andrew Sacks – 97, (top, left, bottom) 98, (lower) 100
William Stegath – 6, 7, 48, 49, 53, 58, 82, 83
Sports Illustrated Magazine – (center) 31, 81

Photos on page 67 appear courtesy of the University Musical Society.

Cover: Gary Quesada '80 BA, Balthazar Korab Studio